People in the Community

Doctors

Diyan Leake

Heinemann Library
Chicago, Illinois

Customer Service 888-454-2279
Visit our website at www.heinemannraintree.com

Designed by Joanna Hinton-Malivoire and Steve Mead
Printed in China by South China Printing Company Limited

12 11 10 09 08
10 9 8 7 6 5 4 3 2 1

Library of Congress Cataloguing-in-Publication Data
Leake, Diyan.
  Doctors / Diyan Leake.
      p. cm. -- (People in the community)
  Includes bibliographical references and index.
  ISBN-13: 978-1-4329-1188-1 (hc)
  ISBN-13: 978-1-4329-1195-9 (pb)
  1. Physicians--Vocational guidance--Juvenile literature. 2. Medicine--Vocational guidance--Juvenile literature. I. Title.
  R690.L38 2008
  362.17'2--dc22
                                2007045073

Acknowledgments
The publishers would like to thank the following for permission to reproduce photographs:
©Age Fotostock pp. **15** (ImageSource), **20** (John Birdsall); ©Alamy (Derrick Alderman) pp. **11**, **22 (middle)**; ©AP Photo (Bill Feig) p. **6**; ©Corbis pp. **8** (Ed Bock), **21** (Graham Bell); ©digitalrailroad.net (Keith Dannemiller) p. **5**; © Getty Images pp. **4** (Panoramic Images), **7** (Steven Peters), **9** (AFP), **10** (Somos/Veer), **12** (Siri Stafford), **13** (Andersen Ross), **14** (AFP), **16** (Pat LaCroix), **17** (Marwan Naamani/AFP), **18** (David Joel), **19** (Mike Powell), **22 (top)** (Panoramic Images), **22 (bottom)** (Mike Powell).

Front cover photograph of a doctor treating a boy in Ghana reproduced with permission of ©Corbis (Zefa/Mika). Back cover photograph reproduced with permission of ©Corbis (Graham Bell).

Every effort has been made to contact copyright holders of any material reproduced in this book. Any omissions will be rectified in subsequent printings if notice is given to the publisher.

Contents

Communities

People live in communities.

People work in communities.

Doctors in the Community

Doctors work in communities.

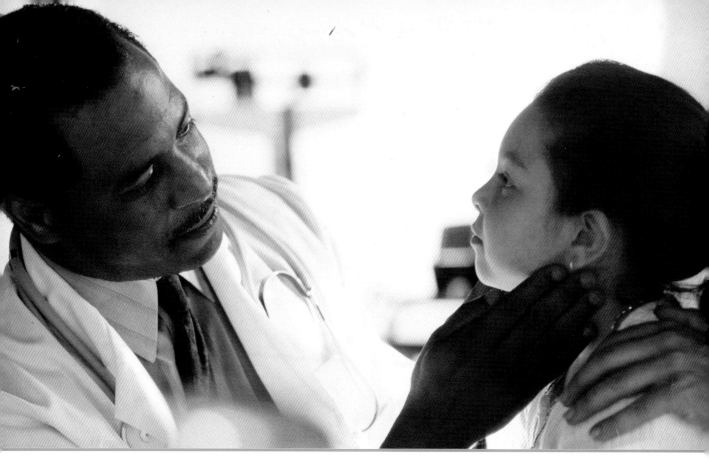

Doctors help people stay healthy.

What Doctors Do

Doctors help people when they
are sick.

Doctors help people when they are hurt.

Where Doctors Work

Doctors work in offices.

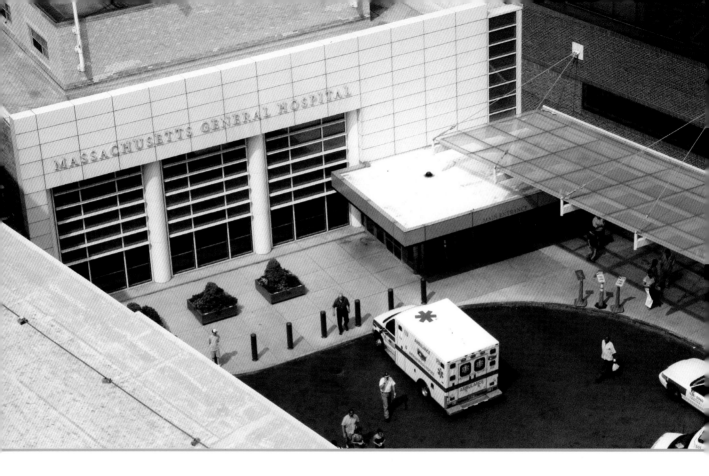

Doctors work in hospitals.

What Doctors Wear

Doctors wear a coat.

Doctors wear gloves.

What Doctors Use

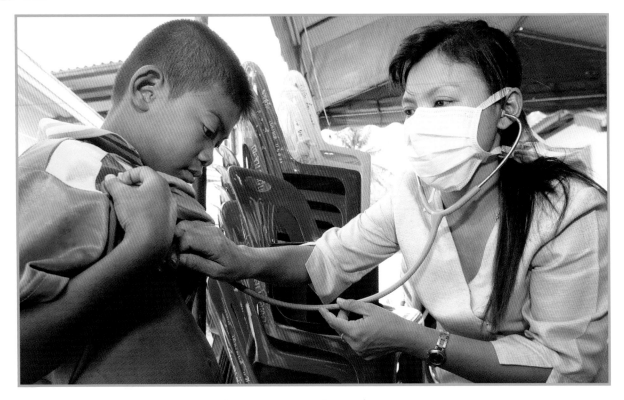

Doctors use tools.

Doctors use their hands.

People Who Work with Doctors

nurse

Doctors work with nurses.

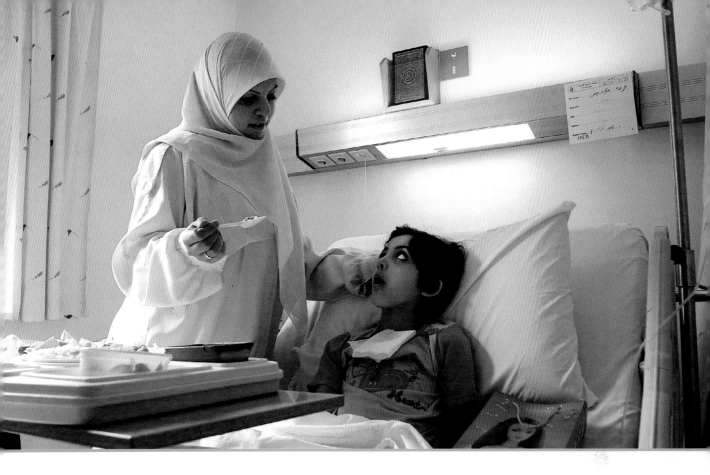

Nurses look after people.

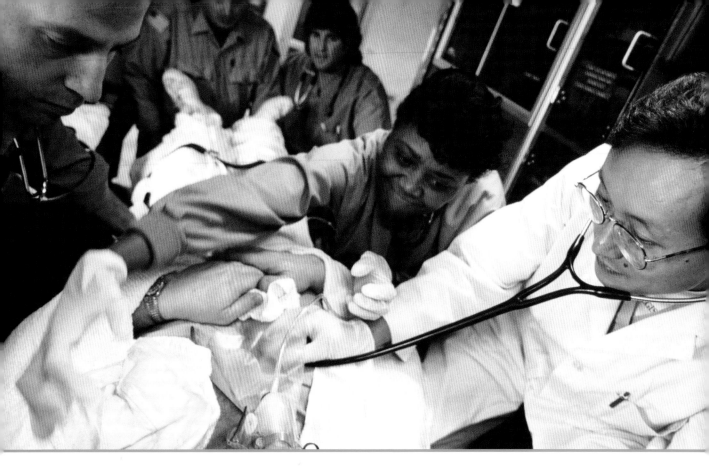

Doctors work with paramedics.

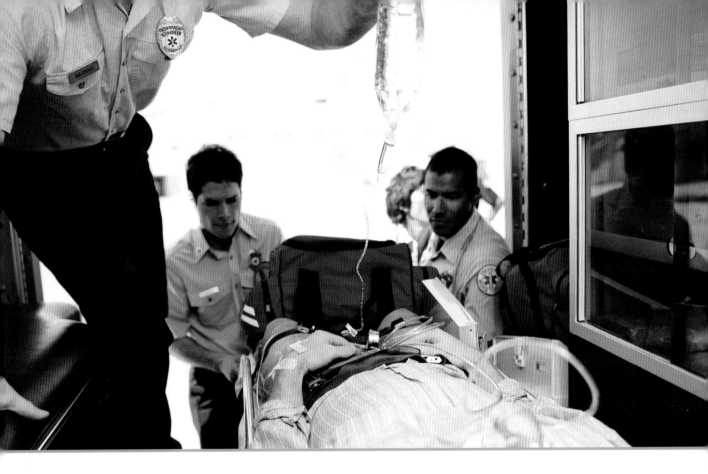

Paramedics take people to
the hospital.

How Doctors Help Us

Doctors help us stay healthy.

Doctors help the community.

Picture Glossary

 **community** group of people living and working in the same area

 **hospital** place where sick or injured people are cared for by doctors and nurses

 **paramedic** person trained to do medical work such as first aid. Paramedics take people to the hospital.

Index

Note to Parents and Teachers

This series introduces readers to the lives of different community workers, and explains some of the different jobs they perform around the world. Some of the locations featured include New York, NY (page 4); Mexico City, Mexico (page 5); Baton Rouge, LA (page 6); Lampedusa, Italy (page 9); Kanchanaburi, Thailand (page 14); and Beirut, Lebanon (page 17).

Discuss with children their experiences with doctors in the community. Do they know any doctors? What is their doctor's office like? Discuss with children why communities need doctors.

Ask children to look through the book and name some of the tools doctors use to help them with their job. Give children poster boards and ask them to draw doctors. Tell them to show the clothes and tools doctors use to do their job.

The text has been chosen with the advice of a literacy expert to enable beginning readers success while reading independently or with moderate support. You can support children's nonfiction literacy skills by helping them use the table of contents, picture glossary, and index.